Learning to Mend

Fly Fishing and Healing

Bill Yearwood

Contents

1. Preface   1

2. Packing Up   3

3. Day 1   5

4. Night 1   13

5. Day2   16

6. Night 2   27

7. Day 3   31

8. Night 3   36

9. Day 4   40

10. Night 4   44

11. Day 5   47

12. Night 5   56

13. Day 6   60

14. The Final Night   66

15. The Final Day   68

1

Preface

Preface

Fly fishing quickly went from a hobby I enjoyed to a desperately needed reprieve. Having served as a combat veteran, a first responder, and now a Registered Nurse, my career path has placed me in direct contact with the heart-wrenching realities of life's tragedies. Each experience—whether on the battlefield, at the scene of an emergency, or in a hospital room—leaves an indelible mark on the soul. Those memories linger, often surfacing when least expected, and it is in the tranquil waters and the rhythmic casting of my line, I find my escape, a chance to process and heal from the weight of those experiences. Fly fishing has become my sanctuary.

Those who choose these professions make many sacrifices. Some sacrifices aren't known until later when we've hung up our hats. But what do we do when the battle is over?

For those of us lucky enough, we find a good therapist, maybe start some medications that help numb us, and get to a point where we can bear getting through life. Those are the lucky ones. Some crash and burn down a path of drugs and alcohol. Some end the pain abruptly at their own hand.

There are other options. These options are not meant to replace therapy and medications, but they can enhance the quality of life for those struggling with mental health issues. One of those options is recreational therapy, specifically fly fishing.

After the military, I white-knuckled life for a bit until finally, spiraling. I achieved and achieved, and when I hit my academic and career peak, I crashed. The relentless drive that had fueled my ambitions began to falter, and I found myself overwhelmed by a tide of panic attacks that hit me like a storm. All the suppressed emotions and unresolved struggles that I had ignored finally came to the surface, leaving me feeling trapped, at the mercy of my mind. The facade of control I had built crumbled, and I was left to confront the turmoil that had been lurking beneath for far too long. The only problem was that I didn't know how to confront it.

Luckily, I found fly fishing and Project Healing Waters. Nature is healing, and there is plenty of science to prove it. Couple nature with an artistic and physical outlet, and it'd be challenging for many people not to get better mentally and physically. Fly fishing is the convergence of all those things, more meditation than sport. The participant must be engaged and present while keeping the fleeting mind occupied.

I hope that a fellow veteran, first responder, or healthcare worker finds this book and sees the benefits that the great outdoors can have. I hope that some of you pick up a fly rod. For Veterans, reach out to your local Project Healing Water's chapter. I'm not promising fly fishing will change your life, but what's the alternative?

2

Packing Up

I t's been a long time coming. Jack sat on an old fold-up stool he'd found in Afghanistan. He sat at the back of his old truck with the tailgate, using it as a table to organize his fly box. He had a can of cold beer that he'd just pulled out of the cooler sitting to his left and a varying array of flies in front of him. Like any good angler, he had dozens of fly variations but continued only to use three or four different ones. It was a hell of a selection, though. His speaker was turned up loud to the tune of Tyler Childers.

Jack had already spent hours sitting at that tailgate, meticulously organizing and setting up leaders. He enjoyed this time alone. He also packed his rucksack, bringing only the essentials, including cigars and whiskey.

This trip had been on the calendar for some time, even though Jack knew it might not happen. His wife had been living in the hospital for the better part of the year, awaiting and receiving a heart transplant, and even though she was home now, her health could require her to be hospitalized again at any time. The first year few months after the transplant had not been easy on her, to say the least.

The year was tough on Jack, too, and everything piled on top of his already troubled mental health. PTSD and anxiety had already dug their claws in him, and the extreme stress of this year did him no favors.

Fly fishing was something that he loved and his only real hobby. He wasn't a professional but good enough to catch a few fish. He at least had enough gear to look like a professional. He didn't have any $1000 rods or $800 waders, but he had economical versions of everything he needed. The prized possession of his fishing gear was a faded and worn Red Sox hat. Jack wasn't a Red Sox fan; he was an avid Braves fan, but he'd bought the hat years ago when he and his combat medic buddies had a wild weekend in Boston culminating with a game at Fenway. He'd taken the hat with him to Afghanistan. He'd also bought a Harvard hoody that he wore while telling everyone in Boston he was a newly 21-year-old medical student. It helped to be a medic and to know some terminology. He was not a medical student. That hoody was a few sizes too small now.

Jack had spent about half the afternoon packing, and the sun was fading. He put his neatly packed rucksack back in the truck. He tossed his beer can in the trash and went inside, spending the rest of his evening watching fishing videos with his wife. He enjoyed them a bit more than she did, but she obliged.

3

Day 1

The sun was just past high in the sky, and it was still warm in the middle of the day. It was mid-October in Georgia, and you could feel Autumn approaching.

The Chenawatchee River is wild and scenic. It is one of the South's great rivers of solitude. Jack picked this river as it was one of the few places he ever found peace anymore.

He parked his aging truck along the gravel shoulder, just off the winding road where the trail to the river began. The drive to this point was scenic, and just down the hill was the last bridge to cross the river until its headwaters up over the state line.

Jack walked down to the bridge and looked out over the water. The river was clear and wide. Water tumbled over dark rocks. Large trees with occasional hints of yellow and red rose along the banks. It had not rained in several days and looked easy enough to wade. They stocked trout this far down the river, and he could see a grouping of five or six stockers in an eddy on the left bank. This section of the river held a mixture of stockers and a few wild fish. As you hiked further north along the river, the stockers disappeared, and large wild Brown Trout roamed.

Typically, Jack would expect to see a few other fishermen casting their lines near the bridge, but today, the tranquil scene was undisturbed; he was alone. It was midweek, and a cold spell was coming, causing many to stay away. For the dedicated angler, this was the prime time to be out on the water.

The Chenawatchee is a naturally flowing river and is not dammed. This means that during the heat of the Georgia summer, even in the mountains, the river can become too hot to fish as it puts too much stress on the resident trout. That would not be a problem right now.

Jack had been eagerly anticipating this trip for months, a much-needed escape from the burdens that had steadily weighed him down. Once, fishing had been his refuge, a soothing outlet that allowed him to connect with nature and forget about the stresses of life—those serene mornings by the water had become a lifeline, offering solace amidst the chaos of his experiences. The traumas he'd witnessed left a lingering cloud over his mental well-being, but fishing had always provided a way to clear his mind.

Over the past year, life had taken a heavy toll on him. His wife had fallen gravely ill, which cast a long shadow over their once bright days. She spent countless nights in a sterile hospital room illuminated by the glow of medical monitors. Each day felt like an eternity as he sat by her bedside, trying to be present for her but often disassociating. Their lives, once filled with laughter and shared moments, now revolved around doctors' visits, treatments, and constant worry. It was a time of trial, testing the depths of his strength and resilience as he navigated the emotional turmoil of watching the person he loved most fight for her health. There was no time for fishing then. Life had quietly settled, and a few days' reprieve was now possible.

Jack took a trip to Colorado a decade ago with his future wife and some old friends. He had never been much of a fisherman but was introduced to fly fishing by his friend Alan, who lived in Grand Junction. Alan taught him the casting basics and helped him catch his first trout on the fly.

Colorado changed Jack. He hadn't yet realized the extent of his struggles with mental health, but he knew that nature brought him peace that he did not have. Returning home to Georgia, Jack and his wife began spending more time in the North Georgia mountains. It was a grand time. They fished. They swam. They camped. They spent hot summer days on calm mountain lakes and cold days along riverbanks, taking it all in.

Jack had been burning the candle at both ends, working full-time as an EMT and attending Nursing school. His and his wife's outdoor adventures became scarce. Jack eventually graduated from nursing school, and things would get better for them. Life would slow down, and he and his wife would have more time together. He was working in an ER while picking up ambulance shifts.

When COVID struck, Jack found himself caught in an unforgiving cycle, working both jobs tirelessly and battling the relentless tide of burnout. The unending pressure chipped away at his mental health. Sleep eluded him; he sought solace in alcohol to quiet the tumult in his mind. Anxious nights became his new normal, with sleep disrupted by the faintest of sounds, his heart racing and breath quickening.

Jack walked back to his truck and pulled his pack out. He unlocked the rod holder on top of his truck and grabbed a fly rod. The trail is flat and easy to hike for the first few miles. It courses along the river, only losing sight of the water for short stretches. Large old-growth trees tower in the woods, and fallen logs decay undisturbed. Dispersed camp sights are dotted along the trail. They were nothing more than small clearings with remnants of a campfire. A few sites had old logs pulled up as benches around hastily made rock campfire rings.

The leaves were nearing their fall peak, with the amber and red-colored foliage well shown. This was Jack's favorite time of year.

After a mile or so of walking, Jack stepped down a narrow footpath to the river. There was dense underbrush between the river and the trail, but the river opened wide, and there were a few good runs to fish. He quickly made it down to the river and laid his pack atop a large boulder. He slipped his waders on and tied on a couple of heavy nymphs. This time of day, he didn't see any fish rising nor a semblance of a hatch. It had been months since he had cast his fly rod.

The bank of the river was full of rounded, dry rocks, and you could see the river almost doubled in size when it rained. In front of Jack was clear water and a deep hole. The bottom of the river was all rock here. Up above the hole was a small rapid formed by the squeezing of the river between large boulders on either side of the river. The river was loud here, and Jack appreciated that. He didn't much care for silence.

Starting at the bottom of the run, he began methodically casting where he believed trout would be. Stocked fish weren't as easily spooked as wild fish but could be spooked. He was careful to wade quietly. The rocks were slick however, and wading quietly could be a chore on this river. Anyone who had spent any time here had succumbed to the pain of cracked knees and water-filled waders.

Jack cast upstream, and the fly gently landed along the far bank. It was deep here. He mended upstream. The Elk Hair Caddis floated gently with a tiny midge suspended well below it on a thin tippet. Jack had the feeling. It was a near-perfect cast, for him anyway.

"Fish on!" yelled Jack. The Elk Hair had disappeared. His rod bent, and the line became taught.

"This is a good fish," he thought.

Jack stripped the line and let the fish run. It was no monster, but with a very light tippet, you can't rush the process. After a brief fight, the Rainbow Trout was netted. Despite its lack of vibrant beauty and marks of captivity, Jack felt an overwhelming sense of joy. At that moment, it didn't matter how the fish looked; the act of fishing filled him with a deep sense of contentment. He relished the connection to nature, feeling some normalcy settle over him.

Jack sat down on the side of the river, leaning back against the boulder his pack was on. He slipped a small flask from the front pocket of his waders and took a pull of dry whiskey. He looked upstream and watched a Blue Heron spread its wings and take flight. He had just noticed the large bird across from him.

Jack could feel the sweat creeping down his back. He changed his waders for shorts and Chacos. The sun stood high. Jack packed his waders and climbed back through the brush to the main trail.

He felt much lighter in shorts, and though his pack was heavy, he enjoyed the physical challenge of the hike. The trail had begun to narrow, and a few deadfall trees had to be traversed along the way. As he neared the site where he wanted to camp, the trail began to incline and decline. Narrow muddy ruts led down to a large sandy bend in the river. On the far end of a large sandy beach was an elevated area where people occasionally camped. There was a rock fire ring in the middle of this site with ashes left from someone before. Jack set his one-man tent about ten feet from the fire ring on a flat spot covered sparsely by pine needles. The sand on the beach below was white and grainy. The earth was dark and moist at his campsite like the rest of the valley. He grabbed his axe and cut some deadfall trees into pieces suitable for his campfire.

Once his fire was rolling, he walked down to the river and filled his water bladder. He boiled some of the water in his small pot. He reached into his pack and pulled out a freeze-dried meal. Tonight was beef stew. It would be tomorrow's meal as well. God willing, he would eat it the day after, too. He poured the boiling water into the meal bag and let it sit. He had a small coffee press and a tin of cheap coffee. He had enough water boiled for it as well.

The freeze-dried meal brought back fond memories for Jack. He leaned against a log beside his campfire and felt an overwhelming nostalgia. The last time Jack had eaten a freeze-dried meal was when he was a combat medic in the 10th Mountain Division. They often had special winter Meals Ready to Eat (MREs) that were freeze-dried as much of their training was cold. Traditional meals could be challenging to eat frozen. The weather certainly wouldn't be below freezing tonight, but a little primitive camping brought him back to a time when he loved who he was. A time he felt invincible.

The sun was setting. It was time to fish.

On the Chenawatchee, the wild Brown Trout were a spectacle. You had to hike for em, and you had to know when to fish. Jack had reached the point of the river where wild trout roamed, and stocked fish were all but absent. A few paces from the river's edge, he sat back on the bank and tied on a large white streamer. The river dropped off steeply from the sandy beach, with a deep cut right in the middle. Dark, bare rock is shown at the bottom of the rapidly flowing water. The light was faded, and Jack couldn't see any rises. He flipped the heavy streamer upstream, and it sunk quickly below the surface. The streamer drifted quickly along the current, and Jack pulled tension on the line to cast again—forward and further this time. He let the large fly drift and swing across the river as it passed him. Nothing. A few more successive casts all yielded nothing. It was dark. The sun had faded, and Jack knew his time was short tonight.

Jack lifted his rod and flipped his streamer farther upstream. As his bait drifted in front of him, he gave a few quick strips of the line. His last strip felt heavy, and he knew he had caught a log or a rock. He kept his rod tip high, hoping to free the streamer.

The rod tip bounced.

He lifted his rod higher and tried to strip some more line.

Nothing.

He turned his drag down and heard the whirl of the reel as the trout took off. It felt like the fish had run a mile, and Jack turned his rod upstream to create tension on the fish. He tried to lead him out of the current. No luck

This is the biggest fish I've ever hooked, he thought.

Though he wasn't religious, he prayed that the fish would stay on. He'd earned a little mercy with the big man, indeed. Jack fought. The fish fought. The fish jumped, and Jack heard a splash.

A monster.

He began to strip line, but he knew the fish was tiring. First, a few feet. Then, he methodically began stripping line in a foot at a time. He knew the fish was close. He felt resistance with every tug. The rod kept a hard bend. It was dark. He could not see where the fish was.

He kept pulling line.

Jack pulled, and his arm shot straight backward past his hip.

There was no more resistance.

He was defeated but not distraught.

He had surely hooked the largest trout he'd ever encountered. He had a broad smile and walked back to his camp cheerfully. He removed his faded ball cap and slapped it against his other hand.

Damn. What a fish.

He stoked up his fire and took a few pulls of whiskey. The fire cracked and popped. The heat felt like a warm hug against the cool night air. He grabbed *A Farewell to Arms from* his pack and read by the campfire. He eventually began to nod and decided to move into his tent. He zipped up in his sleeping bag and drifted off.

4

Night 1

"Boom"
Little Jack heard the cars crashing in the middle of the night. Then he heard his father screaming. He couldn't tell what was being said, but he knew his father was drunk and angry.

Jack and his brother exchanged nervous glances, their hearts racing as they crept toward their bedroom door. They pressed their ears against the door, desperate to catch a hint of what was happening outside, yet instinctively, knowing that opening that door could unleash their father's wrath onto them. The tension in the air was palpable, a suffocating blanket of anxiety that wrapped around them as they stood frozen, caught between the safety of their room and the frightening world just beyond. But there was no escape from the reality unfolding just outside. The crashing sounds continued, punctuated by his father's voice, which grew louder and more incoherent with each passing moment. Tears slipped down Jack's cheeks as he listened. Their father had intentionally wrecked the cars in the driveway into each other. No one remembers why. Then, in a rage, their father came for their mother.

Their dad was a good man sober. Hardworking. Intelligent. He was a do-it-all kind of man who didn't have many limitations. He lived life on the edge as well, racing cars and the drugs and alcohol that came along with it. Jack's mother sheltered the kids from most of this, but she was a victim tonight.

"You fucking bitch, you better open this door, or I'll fucking break it down!" Jack's father shouted.

"You need to stop." His mother pleaded. "Please, god, stop".

Jack heard a loud crack and his mother screaming—pleading for his father to stop. His father had shut the door back after kicking it in. Jack and his brother Andy beat on the door, pleading with their intoxicated father to stop. They couldn't see their father's face, but they knew the look in his eyes. It wasn't rage. It wasn't anger. It was a person not thinking.

"Dad, please—please stop." Jack pleaded. "Please stop hurting mom."

Their mother screamed for it to stop. Jack could only imagine the beating she was taking.

His father eventually went back outside and continued his drunken rage, crashing cars together again. Jack can't remember if or when the police came. He stood nearby, a helpless observer, his mind a foggy haze where details slipped away like grains of sand through his fingers. It was all a blur. His mother was distraught. The strong matriarch of the family could tame their father at times. Not this time.

Jack jolted awake, his heart racing as panic surged through him, a familiar sensation that had become a haunting companion to his restless nights. He was drenched in sweat. The wind howled. He shivered as the wind shook his tent. He grabbed his headlamp and decided to read for a while. Reading could often calm his mind. A Farewell to Arms was a book he'd read before. Hemingway may glorify himself at times, he thought, but he did not glorify war. Jack appreciated that. It was no hero story. It was a man forced to be a man, faults withstanding. He also connected deeply with this story, having been an Army Medic and the main character, Frederic, an ambulance driver. Jack's deployment to Afghanistan was no hero story. For Jack, his deployment had never been glamorous. He served, fulfilled his responsibilities, and returned—not as a hero but as a survivor grappling with the reality of what he had witnessed. It took time for him to come to terms with his experience and to find gratitude in survival instead of glory.

As he turned another page, the words enveloped him, offering an escape and an understanding of the shared burdens borne by men like them.

We go to war with our youth, hoping to be heroes. At some point, we become men and beg to be home. We're gone much longer than we realize.

Soon, Jack was asleep.

5

Day2

J ack slipped on his wool socks. He tugged a snug beanie down over his ears, a shield against the crisp morning air that awaited him. He stepped out into the morning. The wind had been relentless last night, but now the air was cool and the trees still. He gathered a few pieces of wood and got a small fire going. As he sat, he could see his breath clouding, a visible reminder of the brisk morning. The thought of a steaming cup of hot coffee filled him with anticipation, the warmth of the drink warming not only his hands but his spirit as well. He watched the water boil and poured it over the coffee at the bottom of his press. Although he was not comfortable at this moment, he appreciated it. There is nothing like a bit of suffering to ground a man.

Jack reminisced about a time when he searched for Brook Trout on the Upper Chattahoochee. Finding native Brook trout in Georgia is no easy task. One must hike and endure dense brush and steep mountains to land a small fish—an enduring survivor from the last ice age, embodying the untamed spirit of the mountains. Each catch was a victory over the river's challenges and a connection to its ancient lineage.

He'd hiked up a trail along the furthest reaches of the hooch. The trail was easy for some time but eventually disappeared, and you either had to bushwack or wade the narrow river that resembled a small creek that far up. He waded up the river. It was no more than 12 feet wide and ankle deep except for a few small pools and cuts. He had made it up not far from the river's source and heard a loud boom that echoed through the valley.

It was thunder.

Another boom.

And another.

He saw a flash of lightning right on top of him. The wind picked up, and he felt a raindrop.

BOOM.

A flash.

The bottom fell out, and the hot summer turned cool. He knew he had to hike downstream or bushwack, so he chose the stream. He was alone, miles away from his truck. It had taken him hours to get here, and he was scared.

The rain became so hard that he could only see a few feet before him. He hurried down the river as fast as he could.

BOOM.

Another flash.

The river rose. The last thing he wanted to do was bushwack. His only thoughts were

Rattlesnakes and Copperheads.

He wasn't afraid of snakes, but he knew a good bite might mean death far away from help and without service.

What a stupid decision.

Eventually, ankle-deep water reached above his knee. As he struggled against the surging water, the once calm river transformed into a roiling beast, its currents swirling fiercely around him. The chill of the water seeped through his clothing, creeping up his legs and wrapping around him like icy fingers. He fought to maintain his footing, but the relentless current surged with unexpected ferocity, knocking him off balance. He decided it was time to leave the river. He tightened the straps on his pack.

He ran.

Thorns. Brush. Trees.

Boom.

Another strike.

His heart pounded as he ran. A tree could fall. A snake could bite him. Lightening could strike him. He was cold. He watched as large trees crashed and fell.

He felt alive and ran, his arms cut and bruised, but he felt no pain. He was exhilarated.

It took Jack two hours to get back to the truck that day. He returned soaking wet and bloodied, but he felt more alive than he had in a decade. As he sat in the truck, the rain poured, and he smiled. He had made it, and for a moment, he was unsure if he would.

At that time, he felt how he felt leaving Afghanistan, flying in the back of a C-17 and sitting against the wall. As the C-17 cleared Afghan airspace, the pilot came over the intercom to let everyone know.

He let out a sigh of relief. He had made it. He was done.

The feeling he had that day on the Hootch couldn't top that, but damn if it didn't try.

His coffee was ready, and he poured a cup—no cream, no sugar. Steam rose from the cup as he sipped, warming his body.

As his cup emptied, he walked down to the river. The rocks were dark. The water was clear. The sun had not long been rising and was not fully awake yet in the valley. He knew he must have a try at fishing.

He decided to suspend a couple of small nymphs below an indicator. He slipped on his waders and was no longer shivering. He stood on the sandy bank and flipped his line across the river. He started at the bottom of the run and slowly worked his way up the deep pool where he had missed the large trout the night before.

He had cast several times and adjusted his rig. The flies now dragged the bottom, and the indicator slowed.

The indicator disappeared.

The rod bent.

The line was taught.

"Splash".

A trout jumped as he pulled and tugged.

It was a good fish.

It fought.

Jack reeled the fish and netted it. It was a wild Brown Trout. Though it was smaller than the prized catch he had lost earlier, this one still boasted an impressive length of about 16 inches. The sharp, translucent fins fanned out gracefully, each delicate edge catching the light and glistening. Its long, slender body arched elegantly. He wet his hands, pulled him from the net, and let him go.

Jack kept fishing and lost track of time. He was now several hundred yards upstream, and the sun was well into the valley. He tucked his beanie into the front pocket of his waders. Above the deep hole in the river where he camped and fished, the river was shallow, and the water tumbled over a series of rocks large and small. He spent some time casting small dry flies around and below some of the larger boulders with some success. The river was full of tiny wild Brown Trout here. These wild fish had deep red spots and vibrant colors. They fought ferociously.

When Jack returned to camp after lunch, his stomach grumbled, and he was sweating profusely from hiking back in his waders. He slipped them off and put on shorts. He let his feet air out. After boiling some water, he fixed a freeze-dried meal and slugged a whole bottle.

It was nice to have a tired body and a calm mind instead of the opposite. Jack's time in the military and career in emergency medicine had left his mind uneasy, and he had a white-knuckled life for some time. His eyes were tired. Dark circles showed below them. His hair was nearly as gray as it was brown. His beard was deep red. Not much gray in it. He was aging fast for a man in his 30s. Life was stressful, and many days, he didn't even know why.

When he got out of the Army, he got divorced and drank heavily. A psychologist had told him he had PTSD when he was getting out. He told that psychologist to screw off.

He started college the summer after he was discharged and dropped his first chemistry class after nearly failing it. For a man going through a divorce and drinking every night, academic success wasn't an option. He spent the rest of the summer getting his shit together.

Things went well for a few months before his newly found easy life began to take its toll. He was developing an overwhelming sense that he had not done anything with his life and was continuing to do nothing. He needed a purpose, and he needed to sacrifice to feel like he was somebody. That need to sacrifice became a theme for him. He passed all his classes that fall semester and learned that history and philosophy were more of a hobby for him than a valid pursuit. He switched back to biology and began doing exceedingly well in classes. He got a job working in an ambulance and found a real passion for healthcare. He wanted to prove to himself that he could save lives. Jack needed to know he could perform under pressure.

After finally landing a job in a 911 ambulance, he got his chance. Quickly, he knew that he had found his niche. He studied relentlessly, and college became easy. Nursing school, though time-consuming, seemed easy enough as he was genuinely passionate about what he was learning. Jack knew that every bit of knowledge he obtained could be used to save a life.

Life started happening at warp speed. One day, he went to sleep. The next he woke up, and a decade had passed. He had proven to himself time and time again that he could perform under pressure. He had been a part of saving many lives, from babies to the elderly. He helped bring people into the world and did everything he could to stop them from leaving it. All of this took a toll. During that blur, Jack had also lost his father and oldest brother. He'd also watched his other brother struggle with addiction. He'd also watched his wife battle with heart failure that eventually led to a transplant—a long journey.

Everything added up.

His passion for saving lives slowly began to fade.

Sleep was a luxury not often obtained. After years of being woken up in the middle of the night for emergencies, how could you sleep? He had lost his peace. He had lost himself. Now, he was afraid of losing his mind.

Nature had become his only solace. Fly fishing helped slow his mind as he focused on the rhythmic nature of it. You had to commit yourself to the present to catch a fish on the fly. You had to feel your cast. Keep your wrist straight. You had to pay attention to the water's speed—the bubbles' flow. You had to see what insects were around. Were there any rises? Were there any fish that you could see? You had to evaluate the hydrology of the water section before you. Trout needs a few things to survive. Protection. Oxygen. Food. You would find fish if you could find a place with all of them. You needed fast water for food and slow water for the fish to not tire themselves out. Fast water next to slow water is your friend, and the bubbles tend to flow along where these differing currents meet. Seeing all this requires you to focus and be present where you are. For those who have served in careers wrought with trauma, you know that being present presents a big challenge. You always look forward, never back. You get by.

The only time Jack had felt this presentness and calm was during emergencies. A fast ride in the back of an ambulance required this same focus. You had to be fully attentive to the dying patient, feeling their skin and pulse.

Weak? Strong?

Fast or slow?

Is skin cool or warm? Pale or pink?

You looked at the monitor.

Does the machine's blood pressure match the perfusion I see? Is the blood warmer ready yet? How does my IV flush? How far until the hospital?

In these moments, all the racing thoughts of the mind line up. Everything makes sense. You are genuinely present. The only problem is that it gets harder to calm down, and the mental chaos gets worse each time this happens. You don't realize it, but months or years later, you know that the slightest surprise drives your heart and mind in a rush. A small bump in the night makes your body send a rush of adrenaline that keeps you awake for the rest of it.

Fly fishing allowed for your thoughts to line up. It allowed him to be present and didn't require a comedown. There was not much adrenaline—just peace. Just focus. Jack didn't realize at first what fly fishing would mean to him. He knew he enjoyed it but didn't know he needed it. He realized that when he fished one day with Project Healing Waters.

If you don't know what Project Healing Waters is, you will find that it is a non-profit that helps veterans heal through fly fishing. Jack went one day in late winter with a local North Georgia chapter. He had never been with them and didn't feel deserving of an opportunity to go on a free fly-fishing trip. He had friends who had died. Friends who had been injured. He had friends missing limbs. He had it good and only had mental struggles and honestly did not feel that he should go fishing with the group. With encouragement from the group leader, he went. That day would be life-changing.

The week before this trip, Jack had dropped out of graduate school. He had a full ride to Emory University and was already living a white-knuckle life. He did well and met the expectations set forth for him regarding his scholarship.

He began struggling with panic attacks during this time, and they became persistent and overwhelming. Jack didn't know what to do as he had never, in his mind, really struggled with his mental health. Everything culminated during the beginning of his second semester. He walked down to the creek at his house and, for the first time, honestly thought about ending his life. He sat down at the creek for a time, and when he walked back up to his house, he called Emory and dropped out that day. He didn't know how he was going to fix his mental health, but he knew he had to. The following week, Jack went fishing with Project Healing Waters.

The veteran group that went fishing that cold March Day was a mixture of Vietnam and GWOT veterans. The older men had built a fire, and they all stood around it, prepared for the day of fishing. Some guys were new to fishing, and some, like Jack, had enough experience to do a little fishing independently. Several guides from the North Georgia mountains had volunteered to fish with them that day, and it was a great experience. For Jack, spending time with other veterans was something he needed. One older man had been a Green Beret in Vietnam and gave all the young guys well-intentioned crap. The older man sat in a chair on the side of the river, commenting on the poor techniques of the new guys in front of him. He looked at Jack.

"Son, you gonna catch a fish today or just wade around freezing your ass off?"

Jack had heard the old man was a real warrior and had survived being shot down several times in Vietnam. He had also fought a long battle with cancer.

"I'll drag your old ass down here with me," Jack snipped.

The old man laughed.

"Try this fly, son. It'll get you one".

Jack nodded and took the small brown fly. "Thank you."

Jack had trouble catching a fish that day. He missed a few but found out he wasn't the fisherman he thought himself to be. He warmed up by the fire and sat by the old man by the river.

"How you doing, son?". The old man looked down from his chair at Jack sitting on the ground below him.

"I'm having a hell of a time. Thank y'all for all of this."

"You're welcome." The old man patted Jack on the shoulder. "Now, how are you doing?"

"I'll be alright. That's all we can be". Jack smiled.

The old man grabbed a fly rod next to him and handed it to Jack.

"Let's get you a fish".

Jack stood on a small dock where they were sitting and began casting his fly. After a few tips from the old man, Jack had a massive trout on the line. The old man coached him for a few minutes and netted the fish. They smiled and high-fived. Jack felt good.

The hours passed, and all the guys spent a few hours fishing and learning from the volunteer guides. Toward the end of the day, a few of the guys started leaving. Jack stuck around and helped gather up equipment. Another Vietnam vet called Jack over to his truck. They sat on his tailgate. This man had been an Airman in Vietnam and had suffered a traumatic brain injury. The man pulled a small bottle of whiskey out of his fly bag and handed it to Jack. They sat there for a while, sharing the bottle and stories; for Jack, today had been like spending a day with your grandfather. The exception is that your grandpa was a badass who fought in Vietnam. Jack had lost his father and both grandfathers. His maternal grandfather was an avid fisherman, but by the time Jack came around, working as a beat cop had taken a toll on his grandfather, and he couldn't do much fishing.

Jack got an experience he hadn't known he had longed for, all the while leeching out some of the pain and anxiety he had accrued in the war and EMS. Fly fishing was no longer a hobby. It was a necessity.

Jack pulled his food bag up high in a tree and tidied camp. He poured water over his fire and zipped his pack up in the tent. The sun was still high. He stuck a bag of jerky and pistachios into his sling pack beside his whiskey flask. He grabbed his rod and followed the trail north. After a couple of hours, Jack made it a good way upriver. He had fished a few runs along the way. The trail had become more difficult but was still there.

Jack sat on the edge of the river as the sun began to lean in the sky. He had not seen anyone all day and knew he wouldn't now. Where he sat was a rocky bank covered with water whenever it rained. It was beginning to cool, but the rocks were warm. About 10 feet from Jack, he saw a snake lying on a small boulder. He walked over to it and heard the buzz of a rattlesnake. At the same time, he realized what it was. A Timber Rattlesnake. This was the first one he'd seen in Georgia in the wild. It was beautiful. Its tail was dark black. From its head down, it was a dull brown with black chevrons and a copper stripe down its back. He was curled up and buzzing.

Well, this makes the day.

Jack admired him for some time.

He fished his way back to camp and had an evening similar to yesterday.

6

Night 2

This Chinook helicopter ride was different than before. Jack had ridden in one many times during training, but this would be the first time in Afghanistan. He was tired and cold. Jack was a medic attached to an infantry platoon in the 10th Mountain Division. This moment marked a significant shift. While he often wore a confident grin in training, today, his expression was sobered by the reality that this was his first time in a combat zone. His platoon had been told early in the day that they would stay at a forward operating base for the coming months. This means their deployment would be largely uneventful and disappointingly dull. He'd waited almost two years to deploy. Training, running, learning. He wanted a chance to prove himself as a medic.

Late that night, they were told their plans would change. Their new mission would be sending them to a combat outpost named Baraki Barak (BBK for short), a dozen or so kilometers away. It was not a far distance but only accessible by air as the roads were laden with IEDs. With short notice, the platoon packed their gear and shuffled to the flight line with everything they could carry. Jack overdid it a bit, as any medic on their first deployment would. He'd packed what

felt like 100 pounds of medical supplies and his regular gear. The few
hundred-meter walk to the airfield had all but kicked his ass.

Jack was sitting in front of the helicopter next to the door gunner.
He was soaked in sweat as they took off but would soon be freezing
as the cold air ripped through the gunner's window. It was utterly
dark and loud. He'd lost his earplugs in the rush of packing. This
almost certainly contributed to his tinnitus in the coming years. They
climbed into the sky as fear and thrill danced together in Jack's mind.

The Chinook landed hard. The flight was much shorter than an-
ticipated. The platoon quickly grabbed their packs and uniformly
hurried off the bird. They huddled about 20 feet behind the Chinook,
and all appreciated the heat from the rear thrusters. The birds took
off. It was cold. Damn cold. The platoon gathered their bearings and
watched as their platoon leader met with a few men who approached
us. It was the commander and team leader from a detachment of
SEAL Team 3. Jack and his platoon will provide them with support for
the coming months. The SEALS showed the Army guys where they
would be sleeping. It was dilapidated plywood shacks with sandbags
covering their roofs. Their platoon of 20 or so men piled into their
shack, which wasn't quite big enough to fit all of them comfortably.
They saw more buildings but wouldn't realize until morning that
many of them were severely damaged from incoming mortar fire.

Primitive wood frame bunks were topped with twin mattresses that
had seen better days. It was close to 2 am. Jack unpacked his gear and
laid in his bunk by the door. There was no heat, but it was warm
enough inside his sleeping bag to get comfortable. A couple of years of
cold weather training had made any cold tolerable with the right gear
and knowledge. A line in the *10th Mountain Song* says, "In the heat or
cold of snow..."

As Jack lay there, he was tense—a tightness wrapped around his chest like a vice. The memory of last night's mortar attack still echoed in his mind long after the dust had settled. The forward operating base had felt like a fortress, with its high walls and menacing guard towers, but out here, in the darkness of this secluded place, the shadows were alive. You felt like you were much closer to where the war happened.

Jack pointed his rifle towards the door and laid it beside him on the bed.

"Boom"

The building shook.

The hell was that?

"Incoming!" a voice yelled loudly.

As quickly as the men drifted off, they were shocked awake. Half-dressed young men raced to the makeshift bunker beside their shack, rifles in hand. Hell, they were boys, mostly. Jack slipped on his crocs and hurried out, careful not to seem too scared. He checked on the men in the bunker and ensured everyone was there. No one was injured.

No other shots would be fired, and after a few minutes, they returned to their racks for a semblance of sleep. For the leaders who had been on multiple deployments, this was routine. For the new guys like Jack, they'd be up for a while. He made a stop by the latrine. It was a three-wide outhouse without doors. A piece of plywood with a hole in the middle covers a metal barrel that would be cut in half. This is where you did number two. When they filled up, you poured diesel fuel into them and burned them. In the next few days, the men would receive incoming fire while doing just that.

Jack laid down, and sometime later, a rat scurried across him.

"Well, he was here first, I guess," Jack thought.

There was an undertone of fear covered up by youthful pride. Welcome to the war.

7

Day 3

I t was bitterly cold this morning, and Jack would be sleeping in if not for the hard ground. He winced as he slowly sat up. His hair was messy, and his bushy red beard was pressed down on one side. His eyes were tired. Jack woke again feeling like he had been in a fight all night.

After getting dressed, he decided to stock up on firewood. *Damn, it's cold*, he thought as he begrudgingly collected wood.

Jack knew the fishing would be slow this morning. He used the morning to tidy up camp, build a fire, eat breakfast, and, most importantly, make coffee. He hadn't always loved black coffee. There was a time in his life when a splash of coffee into a cup of cream and sugar would do. That changed in Afghanistan. The coffee made by the foreign nationals working there was a thick black sludge. No amount of cream or sugar could tame it. When Jack finally had some real coffee again, he didn't need the cream or sugar. He appreciated it for what it was. He became somewhat of a coffee connoisseur overseas and even tried espresso. That turned out to be a terrible experience. He misunderstood the "barista" and ordered a 12-ounce cup containing only espresso. After 24 hours of being wide awake with his heart racing, he finally slept. It was his last night in Afghanistan. He slept until a barrage of mortars violently shook their sleeping quarters and woke them up.

The loudspeakers blared, "incoming, incoming, incoming!"

Admittedly, he was so tired that he rolled onto the floor and hoped for the best. In the end, it worked out.

Two nights later, he would be home. His journey home had begun days before with a Chinook helicopter ride back to a forward operating base. His next leg was a C-130 to Bagram. After a few days in Bagram, he was on a C-17 back to Romania, and then he took commercial flights from Romania to Germany and then home to Ft. Drum, NY. Romania was notable for its rich chocolate milk in the base dining facility and the black and white cat that bit Jack. A sign read, "Do not pet the black and white cat." When he got home, he hugged his soon-to-be ex-wife and didn't think much about the days before. He just loved black coffee.

His camp was well set, the fire roaring. Sunlight crept in through the canopy. Frost still covered the ground. Jack decided to do some reading. He thumbed the pages of the same Hemingway novel he'd read the days before. He escaped. He went back to a simpler time as the pages flipped. No anxiety. A time when he could let go of his worries. When nothing much stuck to him. Nowadays, if he wasn't distracted, he was uncomfortable. He hated that and searched for ways to return to who he was. Fly fishing helped, and it had become most of what he wanted to do when he could. He had to do his best to stay out of his head. Fly fishing allowed that. Nature allowed that. It was always the nights that got him, even in nature. He was thankful for the days.

The sun was now high, and it'd warmed up a bit. It's still cooler than yesterday, but not painfully cold anymore. Jack grabbed his sling bag full of flies and tippet and grabbed his rod. He hiked upstream and had decided earlier to fish a small tributary stream. The tributary rose quickly through a steep holler with many waterfalls, creating deep pools and short runs that looked promising.

Jack tied on a small Elk Hair Caddis and a size 20 Zebra Midge as a dropper on a long, thin tippet. He hiked a ways up, working a few runs. He'd caught a few small Browns. They were beautiful fish. Wild. Sharp, translucent fins. But they were small. He'd been told some time ago that trophy Brown trout roamed these waters, and nothing less than such would be acceptable. As a matter of fact, he'd run into a Fisheries Biologist last year who'd shown him quite a few pictures of 20-inch Browns that had been caught in the tributary in the past few years. It was the time of year for it. With any luck, spawning fish would be cruising where Jack was fishing.

The river was tight here, though not unfishable. There would be little false casting but plenty of room to stretch out some roll cast. He reached what would be the best run of the day.

Hot damn, this is it.

He crept up behind a few large rocks and leaned against the biggest, where he had a good vantage point. He saw the biggest fish he'd personally seen in this area. He saw the trout swimming lazily along the bank, dipping in and out of cover. It wasn't rising, just swimming. Jack was careful in his movements and knew he would only have a few chances at this fish. He had a wide grin on his face. He locked in.

His first cast fell short. Fortunately, it was short enough that the large fish didn't notice.

He cast again. Closer. Still short.

The trout was still unphased. Jack stepped back momentarily to plan what he knew would probably be his last attempt. He'd already gotten lucky twice. There wouldn't be a third time.

He cast.

He watched.

The burly trout jumped away back to the safety of its enclave.

Jack watched.

The fish was gone.

He let his fly drift downstream and watched in disbelief. The cast was perfect. The flies landed smoothly, or so he thought. The giant he had stalked won this bout. Nonetheless, Jack was excited. He knew big trout lurked in these waters and was more motivated than ever to catch one.

As Jack's heart rate returned to the baseline, he could feel the ache in his back and the soreness in his legs. He'd hiked up much further than he'd realized and silently dreaded the hike back. He was thankful it was mostly downhill on the way back to camp.

The walk back seemed shorter, and Jack quickly returned to camp. He was warm and could feel the sweat running down his back. He knew if he didn't get dry and have a fire going, he would soon be very cold. He sat his pack down, stripped off his last long-sleeve layer, and quickly cooled off. Soon, he dried off. There was plenty of dry wood piled up. Jack got the fire going and stoked it up till it was roaring. He boiled some water and made a freeze-dried meal. He'd also packed some jerky too.

After dinner, Jack took a few long pulls of whiskey. He looked at the fire, and the stars began showing in the dark blue sky. Jack felt an unexpected clarity wash over him as the flames flickered and the night deepened. He had been living in a haze, racing from one moment to the next, always chasing something beyond his grasp. But here, in the stillness of the evening, he could breathe. He then looked down the river he could see below. He just took it all in for the first time in a long time. He just looked. He was present.

This was a momentous moment for a man living life with the pedal to the metal. Jack felt something welling up inside him, and quickly, it spilled over. He burst into tears, crying with his whole body. Pain. Fear. Suffering. Grief. It all came out like a 100-year flood. He didn't know what he was crying about. He didn't know why. He just needed it—a release from the weight he'd carried too long.

After a few minutes, he wiped his eyes and closed his whiskey bottle. He felt relaxed and a bit tired. There would be no fishing tonight. He sat by the fire till it died down, reading a little. The sun had and retired for the night, and so would Jack. As he turned in for the night, Jack felt lighter, unburdened. Tomorrow would bring new challenges, but for now, he allowed himself to drift off into a peaceful sleep.

8

Night 3

The tones dropped. The booming voice came over the intercom requesting a response to a single-car motor vehicle accident. It was 1 am. It was fall, and the nights were cool, much like now. Jack and his paramedic partner jumped into their ambulance, still half asleep. They radioed the dispatcher and let them know they were en route. Dispatch gave a little more info about the type of vehicle involved and which side of the interstate it was on. They were in a rural area. The roads were empty at this hour. They were about five minutes from the wreck.

The dispatcher radioed, "The Deputy on the scene is requesting that you step it up and provide an ETA."

Jack's stomach dropped. He knew this would be bad.

He pushed his foot harder into the pedal and focused on the dark, winding roads. Adrenaline coursed through his veins, sharpening his focus. The lights and sirens were on. He was fully awake. He felt a weakness in his knees.

"Where did this feeling come from?" he thought.

When he arrived on the scene, Jack blocked the remaining lanes of traffic with his ambulance. Only the deputy and Jack's ambulance were on the scene. His paramedic partner walked over to the truck to check on the patient. There was only one patient. Jack saw that the truck had crossed over the median and flipped several times as he walked up.

One patient.

The truck was flipped onto its crushed roof. A semi-truck driver was standing close by and shaking. He was tearful and asked several times if the driver was okay. Jack had already seen the mutilated arm hanging out the broken window, hanging on by threads of tendon that did not look real. A puddle of blood saturated the asphalt around the nub. The driver was folded in half and probably died on impact.

"They passed, sir. Let's get you back to your truck and off the road. I'll walk with you," Jack told the truck driver.

The trucker nodded.

The police, the fire engine crew that had now arrived, and the ambulance crew combed the median and ditches around the accident to ensure no more passengers. Nothing.

They all met back at the car as a rendezvous point. The radio was still playing twangy 90's country.

The firefighters had begun cutting the dead driver from the vehicle. The truck driver had returned and was watching.

Jack approached him and said, "You don't want to see this boss; you

don't forget some things.

The truck driver acknowledged Jack and returned to the truck.

They finally freed the body and pulled it from the wreckage. Jack held the shoulders, and they laid the body in the coroner's bag. The severed arm brushed against Jack's forearm and left a streak of blood.

Damnit, he thought.

Jack awakened from his slumber to a loud thrashing of the tent. The wind had picked up and was blowing hard through the valley. His heart was pounding. He was sweaty. He felt like he had been in a fight. He unzipped his tent and leaned out. He could see the shadows of the trees swaying in the wind. He was nervous. He stepped out, slid on his Chacos, and crossed his arms tightly in the cold wind. Jack knew that wind made sleeping below trees in the forest less than ideal. He had looked for widow makers before setting up the tent. He was now second-guessing if he had seen any or not. Either way, he was awake. He slipped his shoes off and crawled back into his small tent. It was nice to slide into a sleeping bag and start warming up. His water bottle sat next to him. He picked it up to take a large sip. He held it and looked at all the stickers he had acquired over the past few years.

The first thing he noticed was a 10th Mountain Division sticker. It showed two red crossed swords; above them, a bold tab displayed the word "Mountain," a reminder of the rugged training and camaraderie he shared with fellow soldiers. Memories flooded back to his time spent honing his skills for the unforgiving terrain of Afghanistan. He found himself yearning for the company of his comrades, the bonds forged in hardship, and a sense of purpose he felt had slipped away.

The next sticker he noticed was a Colorado Weedery sticker, stirring a wave of nostalgia. He remembered how he never cared much for weed; it always made him feel anxious. Yet, the memory of that small wooden dispensary across from his favorite brewery in Palisade, CO, brought a smile to his face. Palisade sat between two monoliths. Mt. Garfield loomed majestically to the north, its arid flat top towering above. To the east, the flat expanse of the Alpine Grand Mesa, where he first learned the gentle art of fly fishing. In those moments, he felt alive, connected to something greater than himself. He loved that place, and it was as if time stood still there.

He turned the bottle in his hand and looked at the stickers on the backside. He had a Combat Medical Badge (CMB) sticker right above a sticker of a large Brook Trout. The CMB was the smallest sticker on the bottle. The Combat Medical Badge, an emblem of courage awarded to Army medical personnel like Combat Medics, symbolized their critical role on the battlefield—rendering aid under the harshest conditions. For many, it was a source of immense pride, a token of bravery, carrying the weight of harrowing memories. Jack, however, felt a compelling indifference toward the badge. He hadn't truly earned it; it was bestowed upon him as a blanket acknowledgment during a chaotic moment of enemy mortar fire in Afghanistan. His heroic act of care, a mere inquiry of "Hey, you good?" echoed in his mind—nothing grand, no dramatic rescue or life-saving intervention.

After being awarded the medal, he stuck it into a plywood wall on a building in Afghanistan. He put the sticker on his bottle years ago to remind him of needing to do more to prove himself. At this point in his life, he was okay with what he had accomplished and was proud of his service again. There were many more stickers on the bottle.

Jack sat it down and picked up *A Farewell to Arms*. The spine cracked slightly as he opened it. He unscrewed the cap of his flask and took a long pull from the whiskey inside. The cold liquid slid down his throat like fire. It burned, but in an oddly comforting way, a slight reprieve from the chill in the air and the whirlwind of thoughts in his mind. Soon, his heart was no longer racing. His breathing had slowed. Jack read and drifted off again.

9

Day 4

Rain ticked against the tent, and Jack awoke quickly with a gasp. He caught his breath and remembered where he was. The rain was coming down hard. The tent walls felt incredibly close together this morning, and despite the rain, Jack had to get out. He put on his rain and stepped outside. He opted to delay breakfast and coffee this morning until the rain stopped. It was cold rain, but it was still warmer than yesterday. It would be a good morning to fish. He pulled on his waders and walked down to the run below his camp.

This must be the best run on the whole river, Jack thought.

The water was flowing fast and murkier than usual. Jack tied on a big, ugly streamer. He stood for a while and watched the rain hit the water. He took it all in. The persistent rain and churning river stirred up distinctly earthy smells that signified a southern Appalachian stream. This kind of weather keeps most anglers away, but Jack loved it.

He started in the middle of the run, casting far across and letting his streamer swing on a tight line. As the streamer aligned with the river, he gave the line a few quick strips. Rain dripped off his oilcloth hat, and his hands were freezing. This was it. This was the day he was going to catch that big brown. He felt it.

He cast, swung, and stripped, methodically moving upstream. He did his best to keep the heavy fly from clunking into the water, though he hadn't mastered casting streamers yet. Then, finally—it happened. As the fly swung, the line went taught, and the rod tip bent. Jack set the hook and bent the rod upstream to hold heavy pressure. Today, he had a heavier tippet and felt more confident leaning into the fish. The rod bowed heavily. He saw a large flash in the deep in the water.

It was the fish.

It was HIS fish.

The fish ran, and the line peeled off the rod. The big brown gave Jack's old five-weight rod all it could handle. Jack did his best to keep pressure, more worried about his rod choice than his tippet choice. He lightened his drag. The fish ran. He occasionally caught glimpses of the beast, and he got more excited each time. He wasn't even sure his small net could contain it.

Jack's hands were no longer cold. He didn't notice the rain dripping coldly on his neck. He reeled when he could, and the fish ran when it wanted. It was a strategic fight. It's more like a dance, with fish and anglers working in tandem as they complete their moves. Reel. Run. Reel. Run.

After what seemed like an eternity, Jack gained more ground than he'd lost. He was going to get that fish today. His shoulder was growing tired, but he was nowhere near exhaustion. This was no "Old Man and the Sea" type fight, but it was brilliant. Jack had the fish a few yards away and had already begun planning how he would net. He was moving the fish into the slower shallows towards him.

Jack reached behind to grab his net that was hanging off his sling pack. As he turned back, he didn't realize he'd let pressure off the fish—the pain of a barbless hook. His rod was no longer heavy when Jack steadied forward with net in hand. He was defeated. He reeled his fly in and hooked it to the butt of his fly rod, and just stood there. He was in disbelief.

This wasn't a battle for a few days with a large fish. This culminated years of hard work and research on Jack's part. He has been given a start in fly fishing by his buddy Alan in Colorado, but since then, he's done the research and spent many fishless days using trial and error. You'd call it work had it not been so fun. Nonetheless, Jack was disappointed. He felt like he was at a point in his angling life where he should be able to catch a wild fish like this. He thought becoming a "legitimate" fly angler was his next logical step, though he could still only tie the most unadorned flies.

One day, he'd heard an ole ball coach say, "There are no moral victories." Well, maybe not. But this wasn't football; that coach always took things a bit too seriously.

Jack stood in the river, not fishing for long enough that any sensible person would have cause for concern for him. He returned from his almost trance-like state and realized the rain had stopped. No rays of sunshine glittering across the water, but it wasn't raining. It was a good time to walk back up and make breakfast. Or brunch. Or dinner. Whatever it was, it was time to eat and have coffee. Hell, it might be late enough for a bit of whiskey.

It didn't take long to get a good fire and a pot of water boiling. Jack soon had his coffee and breakfast. Today, he didn't feel rushed to keep fishing and decided he'd lay around awhile before going back at it. He even took a short nap, feeling more than comfortable in his waders. The heat of the fire put him out like a dog under a wood stove.

He awoke a short time later. The skies had cleared up, and he had a renewed energy to hit the stream. He shed his raincoat and made his way upriver. He wasn't as upset about losing that big fish as earlier. He was thankful for the experience. He was grateful for all his experiences in life. Some had not been the best, but lessons and opportunities, nonetheless.

He loved being an EMT and an ER Nurse, but he left that behind, knowing what the stress was doing to his mind and body. He was also learning what the stress of his childhood was doing to his body. This past year had offered Jack a chance for introspection, and honestly, it had been downright brutal.

His wife received a heart transplant in the middle of the year and stayed months in the hospital. Apart from the pain and suffering that his wife went through and continues to go through, Jack suffered in his way. He felt guilty even thinking that.

Not only did Jack realize he was constantly anxious and stressed, but he was beginning to see why and was even trying to do something about it. Like any reasonable man, he avoided therapy and medications and leaned into his hobby. It helped.

10

Night 4

I t'd been a hell of a morning already. One cardiac arrest from EMS brought in that was dead. A heart attack. A kidney stone. A stroke. We don't have the staff for this shit.

A grainy voice comes over the hospital radio.

"Medic 1, we are en route with a one-year-old male. Cardiac Arrest. Asystole on the monitor. Unknown downtime. ETA 5 minutes".

Son of a bitch.

Working in EMS and the emergency room, you get accustomed to folks dying. Not kids. Not for Jack. It never got easier.

Jack caught the oncoming ER doctor walking in the ambulance bay and said, "Hey doc, there's an ambulance pulling in with a pediatric arrest."

"Why in the hell is that the first thing you say to me? I mean, what the hell, man?".

The doc stormed off briefly to the lounge and returned with his stethoscope.

As the ambulance crew entered the door, the doc patted Jack on the back.

"Sorry, man, it's just getting hard, ya know."

"No worries, man, I'm with you."

The parents had found the child unresponsive in bed this morning. EMS found him cold but started CPR anyway. Had it been an adult, they would have been pronounced on scene.

The crew quickly switched from the stretcher to the hospital bed. Jack felt like there were 100 people in the room.

The simple and chaotic scene of a cardiac arrest continued.

One on compressions, one on meds, respiratory on the airway. One person documented. The doctor led the show. Several others stood by, waiting for their turn on compressions.

The team worked for 45 minutes. Jack's hands were sore and tired. The young child was pale. His body is lifeless, and his face is underwhelmingly expressionless. There is not as much beauty in grace in death as many hope, especially in a hospital.

The doctor called it.

"Time of death, 1030."

Jack kept pushing hard on the chest.

The doctor reached his hand out, put it on Jack's shoulder, and nodded at him with a solemn look on his face.

"You all did a great job. There was nothing we could do."

Jack felt pain and sadness but couldn't cry. He wanted to. Hell, he yearned too. He tried to get all of his feelings out but couldn't.

The day went on, and I stayed busy.

An urban outdoor enthusiast came in demanding pain medicine for various chronic illnesses that multiple previous ERs had failed to treat. All this according to the patient, of course. After the doctor decided against prescribing another narcotic prescription to the patient, multiple had already been written by other doctors in the past few days. The patient became irate, and Jack took the brunt of it. The older man ripped his IV out and threw it in Jack's face. He was promptly escorted out of the hospital.

Later in the day, a young man was brought in by the police for being high on drugs and hitting a family head-on in a serious accident. This man was okay. The family he hit was not. The young gentleman was in handcuffs with an officer at his bedside. He complained of various ailments, doing his best to delay going to jail for vehicular homicide. After extensive testing showed no serious injuries, the man began fighting staff not to leave. He ripped his IV out as well, a common theme for this day. The difference here is that this man was Hepatitis C positive and knew it. He did his best to get any staff member near him bloody. Luckily, the fiasco only lasted a few minutes, and the man was taken out of the hospital and sent to jail.

Later in the evening, an older lady came in with trouble breathing. She had stage 4 lung cancer and did not appear to be doing well, but it seemed like she would pull through for today at least. She did not pull through, however. Jack cared for her but felt disconnected and numb. He supported the family and put on a façade of empathy. The family appreciated his compassion, but he secretly felt guilty for being disingenuous.

Jack sat at his computer, nearing the end of his shift. He scarfed down some nutter butter he had taken from the patient's stash.

"Did I eat today?"

He had not.

"Hell, have I pissed today?"

He had not done that either.

Jack badged out

11

Day 5

T he air was crisp. Jack could see his breath; even though it was cold, he was drenched in sweat inside his sleeping bag. He rolled onto his left side and grimaced. His right shoulder needed to be repaired for some time, but he wasn't quite ready to let the VA give him a second opportunity to die for his country.

After getting layered up, he started a small fire. This morning felt like a shift from summer straight to winter. Jack only had one thought: *I bet the fish are loving this.*

Jack decided to hike up a few miles to the end of the main trail. The fishing pressure was low there, and the easiest access was the five-mile hike from the trailhead or a shorter hike for those willing to camp out. The breeze was steady, and the river was filling with leaves. The river looked similar up here. It was still wide with good casting lanes, but shallow ripples and skinny pools prevailed.

It was still morning, but barely. Jack set up a dry dropper with a skinny tippet. The water was clear, and these wild browns could even spook themselves. The action started fast, with smaller wild Brown Trout taking midge nymphs with abandon. Cast after cast, Jack pulled in vibrant and angry fish, releasing them gently from barbless hooks.

After catching a dozen fish, he took a break along the bank. The sun was high above now, and it had warmed up considerably. Jack peeled off a layer and ate lunch. Lunch would be an overstatement. Jack ate some jerky and a few large sips of water. He decided to read a little. He appreciated the simple and genuine nature of Hemingway's writing. He wanted to see it as tragic as some do, but it's just life to him.

The light was dim when Jack woke up. His book laid open across his belly. He was parched, and his stomach growled.

Shit

Jack quickly packed and headed back to camp. It was almost dark now, and he would surely be walking back to camp in the dark. Not the worst thing. Not the best. Not intentional. It was long before he stopped. Not far from where he had just left, a husky Black Bear stood in the road.

It blew at him.

He stared.

The old Bear stared back.

Ursus Americanus

The bear was beautiful. He wasn't too old, but he was large, especially for this area, and you could see scars of life on his round face. The bear gave Jack a spiritual feeling that they were much more connected than even Jack could realize. Jack felt scared, but even more so, he deeply respected the beast before him.

Jack reached down at his hip for bear spray.

The bear blew again and turned to head up the hillside.

The bear was gone.

Jack wanted to enjoy the moment, but even more wanted to get back to camp.

How long had that bear been watching me?

The trip back seemed shorter than he expected. He was wide awake and wasn't ready to lay down yet. He kindled up a nice fire and pulled out his journal. He wrote a bit about his day and felt he was much more a man of words than writing. He struggled to capture the feeling he felt running into the bear.

What he did know was he felt. He felt something, even if he couldn't exactly explain it. He felt grounded, connected to where he was. The face of that bear reminded him that there was a lot more to life than the artificial constructs created for us by other men.

Jacked decided he would catch that big trout that broke him off. Just as he had decided this, the old man walked up in the dark.

"Hello, son".

"Evening, sir."

"I was looking to make it back out before dark, but I'm not quite as fast as I used to be. Mind if I sit for a bit to get my bearings?"

"No problem, let me stoke the fire up. Coffee?"

"That'd be great," and the old man pulled a cup out of his bag,

The old man's face was tired and well-defined by lines marking his age. His trimmed beard was white and matched the hair showing underneath his hat. The old man had rolled the sleeves up on his flannel shirt, and Jack could see a faded tattoo with the words "De oppressor liber." This was the motto of the U.S. Army Special Forces. Better known as Green Berets. Jack wasn't Special Forces, but he had the opportunity to work with them many times when he was with the 10th Mountain Division. He respected those men and was in awe of their dedication and professionalism. The title "Green Beret" could tell you more about a man than words ever could.

"Green Beret?" Jack asked the old man.

"Some time ago," the old man said as he grinned. "How bout you?"

"Army, but not Special Forces."

"Thank you for your service," the old man said as he nodded at Jack.

"Thank you too, sir."

Jack poured the old man a cup of coffee.

"Cream and sugar?" Jack quipped, both knowing they didn't have any.

"I'll take mine as god intended," the old man said as he smiled and reached for the fresh cup of campfire coffee Jack was handing to him.

"As will I." Jack sat back on a log by the campfire.

Jack enjoyed the company. He wasn't exactly afraid of the dark, but he didn't love it. At night, his mind raced. He liked the conversation to calm it. He appreciated the company of a fellow veteran; even though the two had fought in different wars, the sentiments were the same. Jack pulled out his flask and took a few nips. He handed it to the old man and obliged with a few pulls.

"Nothing like cheap coffee and cheaper whiskey," the old man joked.

"Yes, sir, only the finest! By the way, the coffee's decaf."

"Hell, that's alright. It's late anyhow."

Jack looked at the old man's rod and noticed it was bamboo.

"You make that?"

"Not this one. An old friend gave it to me."

The old man handed the rod to Jack, who reverently examined it before returning it to the old man. Jack ran his fingers over an inscription on the base of the rod that read, "Remember to mend."

"I've always wanted to build a rod, but I should probably focus on learning to tie better flies first."

"It's an art. For an avid angler, it becomes a necessity. I've built a few myself, but I always come back to this one."

The night was well dark, and their coffee cups were empty. Jack still wanted to fish and invited the old man to come with him. The old man obliged and grabbed his net.

"Not gonna bring your rod?" Jack asked.

The old man patted Jack on the back and said, "Not this time. Let's get you a good one."

The old man and Jack walked down to the river where Jack had fished the past couple of days. Jack had lost that elusive large fish here a few times before but hoped he had all the right answers this time. With encouragement, he switched the streamer for a couple of wet flies. The old man held the net, standing a few feet back on the bank. They stayed quiet. Jack cast, let the line swing and cast. Jack hadn't trout fished at night much and wasn't entirely confident he'd feel a strike. He'd always relied on sight. The old man had reassured that he'd feel the big fish on a tight line swing. He cast, let the line swing, and cast again.

"Good job, Jack," the old man said, strong but softly.

Jack was locked in.

He cast.

The line swung.

"Throw a mend on the next cast. It'll help get those flies down a bit. Let em settle.

Jack obliged and threw a mend upstream as he cast across the river.

The old man spoke again, "A little mend and the flies can settle."

The rod bent forcefully! Jack turned his rod upstream to keep pressure on the fish. Line ran off the reel, and Jack had a large smile. He had him hooked good.

"Good job. You'll have him yet. Let him run and keep pressure." The old man placed his hand on Jack's shoulder as he spoke. "That's it. Let him fight."

It felt like an eternity, but Jack finally started gaining ground. It felt eerily similar now to when he lost the big fish the other day, but he kept hope. He reeled. The fish ran. He reeled. It ran. There were no worries at this moment outside of catching this fish. Life slowed down, and Jack felt a calm come over him. He was excited, but not in the heart-pumping way that he usually was.

Jack was gaining ground, and the fish soon felt like a heavy log. He eventually led the fish into the slower water, and finally, the old man caught it in the net.

"Hell yeah!" Jack exclaimed.

"Now that's a fine trout," the old man said as he shined his flashlight on the beast so he could remove the hook.

The big Brown Trout was well over 20 inches with a butter-yellow belly and glowing red spots. It was the largest wild trout he'd ever caught and certainly the one he'd been playing cat and mouse with for the past few days. He held the dinosaur in the water while it caught its breath. Much quicker than the catch, the fish was soon released. It swam away. Jack and the old man high-fived.

"Couldn't have done it without your help," Jack said as he thanked the old man.

"You had the skills," the old man said as he smiled, "But support never hurts."

"Your turn?" Jack asked.

"Nah, son, that's all the excitement I need for the night. I think it's a little late for me to hike back. I'm gonna find somewhere to set up camp."

"Stay here if you'd like. There's already a fire and plenty of room for your tent."

"Well, that would certainly make it easier. I don't want to impose".

"No sir, stay," Jack said as they shook hands.

The old man returned to camp, and Jack stood by the river for a bit. He listened to the water flow and focused on being present. He felt the cold, damp air against his face.

After walking back up to camp Jack had boiled more water for a meal and offered the old man some.

"No, thank you," and he pulled out a pack of pistachios.

The old man reached into his pack, handed Jack his flask, and said, "Try this."

Jack took a long pull and immediately knew this wasn't cheap whiskey.

He nodded at the old man with a grin.

"Don't be cheap with your fly box or flask." The old man raised his flask.

Jack chuckled.

They stoked the fires and drained their flasks as the night went on. They talked about fly fishing and shared stories of their favorite trips. They also shared lighthearted stories about their military service, the old man having many more stories from Vietnam than Jack had from Afghanistan. A theme the men noticed was that many things changed from one generation to another, but the camaraderie, brotherhood, and battles remained the same. Then, the night went on.

Jack asked the old man, "How are you after all of it."

"Hell, that's a loaded question, ain't it?" The old man said jokingly before pausing for a moment. "Five decades. It's been five decades, and I still wake up sometimes. Five decades, and I still see my platoon leader's face. It's gotten better, but it never gets perfect. It will get better".

Jack knew he hadn't seen the type of war this man had, but the trauma from EMS and Nursing had piled on along with his time in service. He was struggling in his own right.

"What made it better?" Jack asked the old man.

"For a time drinking. For a longer time, adrenaline. I had to hit rock bottom, learn a little about myself, and slowly return to somebody I could live as. I lost my first wife and my oldest son through my actions. My mind raced when it wasn't subdued by alcohol or excited by doing something stupid or dangerous. I fought the world as my mind fought me.

"So, you ask what made it better? Time helped, but I eventually had to accept that I wasn't as strong as I thought and sought help. God helped me, too, but I'm no evangelist."

The old man handed Jack his whiskey. The flask was all but empty.

"I'm rambling, son."

"Hell, I'm listening," Jack said as he looked intently at the old man.

"Your real question is, what can you do to make it better? So, here's some advice from a crazy old man. Take it with a grain of salt. Firstly, talk to somebody. Preferably a professional. I shunned this idea for a long time, and I suffered more for it. Find good friends to talk to as well. Secondly, you found a darkness in yourself. We all have it. You're not crazy. You're not a bad person. Feed the good wolf, as the legend says, and the darkness stays subdued. Don't be afraid of it. Learn from it. Don't contemplate too much on the negative. Learn from the darkness; don't live in it. Live in the light, brother. Force yourself into a life of light. If that means changing people or changing jobs, stay in the light.

"Secondly, ground yourself. Your mind can be your worst enemy; sometimes, you must step out of it. What I mean is to find a way to connect to your immediate present. Fly fishing is an excellent tool for that; whether you know it yet or not, that's why you enjoy it. When you go through the shit we have, you learn to focus on the future and get through what you're going through. That works well for us when we need it but not when we don't. You're living now. Not tomorrow, not yesterday.

"Lastly, life isn't about the catching. It's about the hiking, the casting, the fishing, and mostly, the release. You've spent a lot of time working towards catching a fish like you did tonight. The moment was over in an instant. The joy came from the journey. Live for the release."

Jack nodded, and the men sat in silence for a while. Jack zipped up his jacket and rolled his beanie down over his ears. The fire was dwindling.

"I'm going to bed, Jack. Good night," the old man said, stepping into his tent. "One more thought before I go: don't forget to mend."

Jack laughed, "That mend certainly caught that fish tonight."

"I mean in life, Jack. You caught that fish because those flies had time to settle. They had a chance to get below the surface. Take time. Force yourself to mend. Get below the surface."

Jack mulled over the things the old man had said before walking to his tent.

12

Night 5

J ack's wife had been in the hospital for months. She'd been on the heart transplant list for some time, but her health deteriorated so much a few months back that she'd been living in the intensive care unit. It'd been rough on her, and quietly in the background, Jack suffered in his own way. Days on end were spent in the hospital except for the days when Jack went to work, or the weeks they both had COVID. He was selfishly grateful for those little breaks, as his wife got none.

He watched as his wife was poked and prodded daily as she waited for a new heart. Extensive lines and tubes stuck out of her neck to measure how her heart was doing and to keep a steady dose of medicine that helped keep her alive. Jack watched her struggle. Getting up to use the bathroom was a chore, and the constant beeps and alarms of medical equipment took away any chance for peace. Privacy was also a minimum. Not many understand what it's like to spend extended periods at a hospital and away from home. Apart from the daily discomforts, there is a looming worry about losing a loved one and a careful hope of her receiving a new heart. There's also the guilt of hoping for that, knowing it requires someone else to lose their life and a family to suffer.

Jack and his wife had already experienced the pain of getting the call and it falling through. The come-ups and the letdowns were almost too much for them, but the day finally came.

It was early summer, and the doctor came in to let us know the news. The following day, the transplant would be happening. Jack's heart began racing, and he had difficulty catching his breath. He'd started having issues with his heart racing in the past few weeks, undoubtedly from all the stress and lack of sleep.

He and his wife sat silently for some time, unsure what to say. They were just being together. They called and let all their family know, and before long, the ICU waiting room was packed. Neither of them slept that night.

Jack hoped he'd find something special to say. The hospital had strained their relationship, to say the least, and he wanted to be sure she knew he loved her. A transplant was a risky procedure, and more things could go wrong than right. He tried not to think of those things that could go wrong, but as a nurse, he knew all too well the miracle that needed to occur for her to wake up on the other side of this. He never found the words to say. He thought maybe he'd already learned to let go of her with all the previous scares. He hadn't.

The morning came quickly, and his wife was off to surgery. He gave her a hug and a kiss. She was off quickly as the surgical team was in a hurry. The family moved from the ICU waiting room to the surgery waiting area. It was a much larger area, and it being Sunday, they were all alone. They all sat anxiously, distracting themselves with chess and a little humor. They ordered pizza and sat it below the "no food or drinks" sign. They did their best to stomach some food.

The hours ticked on, and they grasped at any update. The thing about heart transplants is that they can often fail before they start due to a multitude of factors. The surgeons don't know for sure that the donor's heart is viable until they physically see it. Then, it must be meticulously transported and finally brought to the surgical room. It sounds simple enough. It is not.

After it was all said and done, the surgeon came to talk with Jack and the family after almost 10 hours. He was an older man, maybe in his late sixties, and very matter-of-fact. He'd done well over 600 heart transplants, and from what the nurses said, no one worked harder than this surgeon. He never rested.

The surgeon pulled up a chair as the family awaited every word. "The surgery went okay. Everything went as expected. The first 24 hours are critical. She's in the ICU now, and she will be intubated until tomorrow so she can rest. One or two people can visit briefly, but we ask that no one stays overnight."

Jack said, "You said it went well. Is there something specific we need to know?"

"No, everything went as expected. There will be a lot of things to monitor moving forward. She's made it through the surgery well."

The doctor was blunt, but there was comfort in his sureness. It seemed all but routine for him. The conversation lasted a bit longer, with the family asking questions and getting reassuring but simple answers.

Jack got to see his wife for a few minutes. The room was full of doctors and nurses, and she had even more lines and tubes running out of her. She was still sedated, and her face was swollen. She didn't look real. She at least didn't look like herself.

Jack obliged the doctor and went home for the night. He made it home and crashed, sleeping most of the night for the first time in months.

13

Day 6

When Jack awoke in the morning, he heard the fire already crackling. The old man had it stoked up and was already boiling water.

"Coffee?" the old man asked.

"Just a sec," Jack said as he walked over to pee on a tree with squinted eyes. "How much did I drink?"

The old man chuckled, "Enough."

Jack filled his cup full of hot coffee and alternated between water and coffee to get his bearings. The old man reached into his bag.

"Breakfast time!" he pulled out a couple of long Cuban cigars.

Jack obliged, and he was much livelier now.

The men sat around the fire and discussed their past couple of days fishing. The old man had a bit more luck than Jack, mostly because he was a much better fisherman. But luck it was. Jack told the old man how he was sure he'd snagged that fish a time or two but lost him both times for whatever reason. He thanked the old man for helping him catch it.

The men talked for a long time, pausing only to toss wood on the fire. It was another bitter old morning, but the men were comfortable beside the fire with hot coffee, lit cigars, and camaraderie. The two men were from different generations but connected by a bond that most would never understand. The conversation was light for a time, but the old man noticed the tired look on Jack's face. Not a look from drinking a little too much whiskey and sleeping on a hard ground. A weary look from just a bit too much life. Too much stress. Too many days where the mind wired itself to stay in overdrive.

The old man reached out and handed Jack his lighter so he could relight his cigar. Then he asked, "So, how are you doing, son?"

"Hell can't be bad being outside next to a warm fire, a cold river, and smoking a cigar."

Both men laughed and tapped their mugs together in a cheer.

"You're right about that," the old man said as he poured into his coffee cup.

"Ya know, played hell when I got back from Vietnam. Apart from all the bullshit about protesting and shaming returning veterans, I played hell with my mind. It's not something you think about as a young man. Your mind, that is. We go to war with some sense of patriotism. We're not worried about living and dying. We're only worried about being man enough to do our jobs. We certainly aren't worried about losing our minds. So long as we die a hero's death, we ain't afraid. They don't tell you the war begins when you get back home. Hell, the worst part is we don't even realize were still fighting for some time after."

Jack looked intently at the old man as he spoke. He felt the words as they were spoken to him.

"I'm an old man now, and I'm not the warrior I used to be, but every day I fight. Every day, I fight for my mind. There was a time when I got back from Nam', I was the man. I was Green Beret, a Senior NCO, and I had a chest full of ribbons. Within two years of being home and being discharged, I hit rock bottom. I lost my fiancé. I lost my first son.

I lost my self-respect. I lost who I was. My mind raced every day, and it was much worse when I was alone. The only thing I could do to slow it down was drink. And drink I did. I functioned for a while, and I told myself I was okay. Before I knew it, I sat in a motel room alone on New Year's Day in 1978 with a gun in my hand."

Jack felt a lump in his throat, and his foot was tapping anxiously. "What'd you do? How did you get better?"

"My teammate from my ODA knocked on the door. I'd called him the day before, and he drove across the country that night. He made me pack my stuff, and we drove to Western North Carolina, where he lived. He traded me my bottle for an old bamboo fly rod. For the next week, we did what you and I are doing now: catch and release. That was just the start, of course."

Jack topped off his coffee. "Fly fishing has been a big help for me. I love it. It's rhythmic. It's engaging, and the only time my mind feels still outside of a drink. I'm fine until night until the room goes quiet. It gets loud."

The old man nodded in understanding. "It's the start, son. I'd be lying if I said every day was perfect, but you'll get a handle on it if you put in the work. My mind didn't miraculously stop spiraling after a week of fishing. I had to build a lifestyle of peace.

"Men like us, we've found the darkness inside of us. We've all got it, but many people never discover it within themselves. It's a hard thing to reconcile. It's hard to learn that we are capable of dark things ourselves, and you've got to get comfortable with that. It's hard to realize how much control our mind has over us if we don't learn to control it. You've found your darkness, and that's okay. Now, live in the light. Live in the light, knowing that you need the light. You need the good days. You need the days on the river, catching and releasing. Feed the good wolf, as they say."

Tears had welled up in Jack's eyes, and he couldn't find the words to say anything.

The old man continued, "I'm willing to bet that some days you feel downright crazy. You feel like you're losing your mind. I'm telling you that you have a choice in that. You're not crazy. Your mind has been has become accustomed to your experiences. Your mind and body have kept tallies on the bad you've seen. It remembers all the stress you've been under. It takes time to rewire that. It takes time to live in the light. It takes reassurance."

Jack said, "Hell, I haven't had a calm day in five years. Some days have been okay, but my mind takes off as soon as I lie down. But hell, I went overseas, came home, worked on an ambulance, and then in the ER. From mortars waking you from a dead sleep to mangled bodies at midnight. How the hell do I reconcile that? How do I pull away from the darkness of a small child's lifeless body? How do I sleep knowing that at any moment, hell could rain down? How the hell do I pull myself into the light when all I know is darkness? Tell me! What am I supposed to do? How do I get better? How do I learn to care about being alive even a little? Hell—it's not even the bad stuff I can't take. It's anxiety. It's the racing mind and the constant worry. I can't take it. I can't take it, man."

Jack was sobbing. The old man let him have his moment before walking over to sit next to him. He put his hand on Jack's shoulder.

"Learn to live in the light, son. Live in the light. It's going to take time. It's going to be hard. It's not impossible. You will get better."

Jack wiped his eyes and took a few sips of coffee. "Man, I haven't cried like that in 20 years."

"Well, that's probably an issue," the old man chuckled.

"I just want to enjoy the days I have. I want to be present and have my mind at ease. I know I have what should be considered a good life now. I can't get rid of whatever is tormenting me."

The old man took his hat off and sat it on the log beside him. "Swallow your pride and start counseling. Make it a priority. Next, lean into what helps you calm down. You're doing that now. Fish more, but don't tell your wife I said that. Don't drink with a purpose. That's a slippery slope. Ask my first wife." The old man chuckled. "Surround yourself with people on the path you need to be on.

"Most importantly, find a reason to be alive. We aren't meant just to exist. I truly believe that. Use your gift to give back. As a nurse, I'm sure you are already familiar with your gift. And this old man's last bit of advice: it's your responsibility to live a life worth living. You know the things you need to do to be better. To be happier. To be calmer. Do them."

Jack looked at the old man and gave a simple "thank you."

"I'm gonna head upstream to the rock, Jack; I need a bit more time here."

"I think I'm gonna fish around here and head back in the morning," said Jack.

Jack and the old man spent the rest of the morning tidying up camp and at some breakfast. The old man packed up all his gear, and they sat around the fire telling lighthearted fishing stories. The old man had many more, and Jack mostly listened. It was a good morning for them both. Jack appreciated the experience.

The old man went his way, and Jack went his. Jack fished close to camp for a few hours and was successful in swinging wet flies. He didn't catch anything of much size, but he caught more wild trout in as few hours as he ever had. Jack made it back to camp late in the afternoon and spent the rest of his day reading and reflecting. He was at peace for the first time in a long time. Not long after the sun went down, Jack was soon asleep.

14

The Final Night

L ittle Jack sat next to his mother on an old swing, which she had moved to the driveway. He was only about 10 or 11 years old. Jack's mother was a simple woman, and a cheap swing set was her prized possession. She loved rocking in it.

Jack's mother handed him a Reese's Cup.

"Thanks, Mom."

"Love you, son."

"Love you too."

His mother was a tall woman and very fit. Apart from being a beautiful woman, she had a beautiful soul. She was a saint in the eyes of many. Jack's mother grew up poor, and her heart for helping others had grown enormously with the help others gave her. She met no strangers. She turned no one away. She'd love you to a fault and end your life if you hurt one of her children. She was as fierce and strong as she was soft and kind.

Jack was her baby and, in his eyes, her favorite. In everyone else's, he was what one might call a "titty baby." He was spoiled, but it would be alright. The other kids were spoiled, too.

They sat on that swing together, just enjoying each other's company. It was warm but not hot. It was late but not dark. Jack had a full heart and felt plainly at peace. His father walked out and leaned against an old Chevy dually. He had an American flag button-up shirt on. He had a prominent mustache and a happy grin on his face. He was doing well at this point in his life. Jack's dad was a truck driver and a good one. He was gone often but did well to provide when alcohol turned its grips loose of him. Right now, he was doing well, and the family felt that.

Jack's oldest brother, Chuck, walked out. He was tall and slender. He had been a high school basketball phenome. Some bad decisions derailed that, but he was a pleasant young man who stole the spotlight. Everyone loved him. He walked next to his dad and put his arm around him. Chuck was the eldest, standing a few inches taller than his dad at 6'3".

Jack's sister Sarah and brother Andy joined the family at the swing. Sarah was a nerd but lived with the same fire and passion as their mother. His brother Andy was the wild child. Fierce, determined, unbreakable, and a bit of an ass to Jack. At this phase of his life, he had died, his hair blonde and looked terrible. Jack appreciated that.

The family enjoyed a peaceful evening. They sat by the driveway until it was too dark to see. They had dinner and gathered around the TV to watch a movie. Life wasn't always perfect, but Jack and his siblings didn't know better.

15

The Final Day

Jack woke up to the sun shining into his tent. It was cold but not freezing. With the fire going Jack poured more river water into his pot and brought it to a boil. Although he had intended to extend his stay for another day or two, the cold had seeped into his bones, and the thought of a hot shower and a cozy couch became more appealing with each moment. He'd also gotten what he needed from this trip and had enough light now to face some darkness. His wife was still sick, his job was still stressful, and his mind still fought him, but today, he's alright. This would be the last campfire he would enjoy on this trip.

Jack felt more rested than he had in years. He felt a sense of peace and genuine happiness that had evaded him. He looked forward to returning home and seeing his wife.

Life hadn't always been easy, and looking back, Jack can see where much of his anxiety and pain comes from. The most profound pain came when he lost his mother at the tender age of 11. Her absence left a deep void in the family, like a sturdy anchor torn from its mooring, and though the family struggled, they fought to hold themselves together. Jack's father fell a hole into drug and alcohol addiction. His brothers followed. His sister remained strong. Jack still grapples with the weight of his past, recognizing that the scars of loss and longing have shaped the man he is today.

Jack's father died in prison a few years back. He was a changed man but never got the chance at redemption. COVID stole that. His oldest brother died as well. A lifetime of poor choices added to the curse of Type 1 diabetes. His brother Andy got clean, and he and Jack are close again. It was a huge blessing for them both. They are close with their sister as well, who carries on their mother's legacy—the matriarch.

After packing his camp, Jack sat by the fire until the last warm flames faded. He hiked back to the trailhead where his truck was parked. It was a bright, cool day. Along the way, he passed a few fishermen hiking in and stopped to speak with one.

"Catch anything," the fisherman asked Jack.

"It's not the catching that's important," Jack said with a grin.

The fisherman about Jack's age looked at him with a broad smile and said, "You ain't wrong... How's the hike up to rock?"

"I didn't make it up today, but an old man headed up and seemed pretty sure about it."

"Good to know; thanks, brother."

Jack admired the man's bamboo fly rod. "Swingin' wet flies on bamboo? Hell of a throwback."

"Yes, sir, it was the only way my grandfather would have it," the fisherman chuckled. "He passed a few years back, and this is the time of year we'd always take trips. Hell, this is his rod... He found a lot of peace out here; I'm thankful he shared it with me."

"Sounds like a hell of a man." Jack looked at the man agreeably and shook his hand, "Remember to mend."

The fisherman gave Jack a surprised look. "Huh—I've heard that a time or two."

Jack shook his hand, and they went on their way.

Jack finished the hike back with a tear in his eye, though he wasn't sad. He knew this trip was something he needed, but he didn't realize how transformative it could be. Jack went on a simple fishing trip but left some of his burdens in the woods. Nature has the capacity to absorb a lot from us if we're willing to be out in it. He loved fishing. He loved this trip. He knew he had to help others have this experience.

He put his rod in the holder on the roof and threw his pack in the back of the truck. He pulled off his socks and slipped on his Chacos. There were a few drinks left in his bottle of whiskey. He walked over to the trash and tossed it in. His old diesel truck took a few turns to crank. The dirt rose from the road as his tag that read "War in Afghanistan Veteran" disappeared.

Made in the USA
Columbia, SC
16 December 2024

49477038R00045